# KEN GRIFFEY JR.

★

# FRANK THOMAS

**Also by East End Publishing, Ltd.**

BASKETBALL SUPERSTARS ALBUM 1995
SHAQUILLE O'NEAL * LARRY JOHNSON
MICHAEL JORDAN * MAGIC JOHNSON
MICHAEL JORDAN
SHAQUILLE O'NEAL
WAYNE GRETZKY
THE COMPLETE SUPER BOWL STORY Games I-XXVIII
THE WORLD SERIES THE GREAT CONTESTS

Please see the back pages of this book for details on how to order these and other exciting titles.

# KEN GRIFFEY JR.

★

# FRANK THOMAS

**BRIAN CAZENEUVE**

EAST END PUBLISHING, LTD.
SYOSSET, NY

To Anne Cazeneuve, whose love and encouragement can never be appreciated enough, and the memory of Arturo Cazeneuve, whose passion for words (and baseball) I carry on.

## KEN GRIFFEY JR. * FRANK THOMAS

First Printing / January 1995

The cover photo of Ken Griffey Jr. was taken by Robert Tringalli Jr. and supplied by SPORTSCHROME EAST/WEST. The photo of Frank Thomas was taken by Tony Inzerillo.

Cover design by Jim Wasserman.

*Copyright © 1995 by Richard J. Brenner/East End Publishing, Ltd.*

Library Systems and Services
Cataloging in Publication Data

Cazeneuve, Brian.
      Ken Griffy Jr. * Frank Thomas / Brian Cazeneuve.
        p.   cm.

      Includes bibliographical references.
      ISBN 0-943403-32-4

      1. Griffey, Ken, 1969-.  2. Thomas, Frank, 1968-
3. Baseball players--United States--Biography. I. Title.
GV865.G75C39 1994  796.357'092'2--dc20

Provided in cooperation with Unique Books, Inc.

This book is published by East End Publishing, Ltd.,
54 Alexander Dr., Syosset, NY 11791

**For information regarding author visits to student groups, contact East End Publishing, Ltd., 54 Alexander Drive, Syosset, NY 11791. (516) 364-6383.**

# Contents

# KEN GRIFFEY JR.

# 1

# Born into Baseball

IT SEEMS AS if Ken Griffey Jr. was born to play baseball. His father, Ken Sr., was a right fielder on the team known as The Big Red Machine, the powerful Cincinnati Reds who won the World Series in 1975 and 1976. His first toy was a small plastic bat, and the first time he remembers watching television, his mother Birdie was telling him to watch the screen closely so he could see his daddy playing baseball.

When other boys were asking their dads to take them to the park, Kenny was asking his dad to take him to the ballpark.

At age five, Ken Jr. was a sight to see on the Riverfront Stadium infield. He often borrowed his dad's spare hats, but had to wear them backwards because the size $7^1/_4$ gear would otherwise fly off his head. He also felt like a padded football player wearing an enormous uniform shirt that would droop over his pants each time he tried to tuck it inside. Sometimes he just gave up and let the shirt flop over his pants, making him look like a little circus clown.

It was great growing up with the other Reds' children. Little did anyone imagine just how many of them would eventually play baseball for a living. Pedro Borbon's son Pedro Jr. went on to pitch for the Atlanta Braves as his dad had for a decade in Cincinnati. Brian McRae would grow up to become the Royals' center fielder in Kansas City, where he was managed for three years by his dad, Hal, another key cog in the Big Red Machine. Ed Sprague's son Ed Jr. hit a game-winning home run for the Toronto Blue Jays in their World Series triumph in 1992, and Tony Perez's son Eduardo later played for the California Angels. And there were others, such as Tommy Helms' son

3

Tom Jr., who played in the minors for three years, and Pete Rose Jr. and Lee May Jr., who made it as far as Triple-A, one rung away from the big leagues.

Yet while Ken was growing up, all he had to do to see all of these future major leaguers was go to Riverfront Stadium a few hours early and play catch with the other kids a few hours before his father took the field. "The Reds had these annual father-son promotional games that would take place before the real thing," Ken's dad recalled. "I was afraid they'd take us one year. No question, this was the Little Red Machine in waiting."

Soon, Reds' players began calling the two Kens "Junior" and "Senior," and the names caught on so well that even local television interviewers sometimes referred to the elder Griffey simply as Senior.

Junior's fondest early memory is of the summer of 1980, when his dad came up to bat in the fifth inning for the National League in the All-Star Game. Ken was at home in Cincinnati with his grandmother, aunt, uncle, and younger brother, Craig. "Daddy's going to hit this next one out," he told everybody. Sure enough, Ken's dad blasted the first pitch from former Yankees hurler Tommy John out of Dodger Stadium. The National League won the game, 4–2, and Senior was chosen as the game's most valuable player. The next day, Junior went to school and told his classmates he would do the same thing one day.

# 2

# Growing Pains

BECAUSE KEN FELT he had to live up to his father's expectations, he often put too much pressure on himself. As an 11-year-old, Ken was batting in a Little League game and lined a rope that seemed headed down the right field line. It looked like extra bases for sure — until the first baseman leaped and snared the ball. Ken was devastated. It was the first time he had ever made an out. He'd been walked. He'd been hit by a pitch. He'd bunted for a base hit just to show that he didn't have to wallop home runs every time he swung. But this, this out, this was different. Other players made outs, not Ken. He'd played more than a dozen games already, and this was the first time batting against kids his own age that he had failed. Ken felt horrible. He spotted his mom in the stands and motioned her back to their car. He didn't want to speak to anyone — not his coach, not his teammates, nobody. He just wanted to leave.

"Everybody makes outs," his mom told him. "Even when Daddy's hitting his best he still makes an out in two out of three at bats."

Ken wasn't impressed. "Good," he said. "When I make the majors, I'll make a few outs. Now, I don't make outs."

A week before Junior's twelfth birthday, Ken Sr. was traded to the Yankees, where he went on to play for five years. Life was tense in New York. Manager Billy Martin and owner George Steinbrenner, two strong-willed personalities, often created a very hostile atmosphere. One afternoon in 1983, Senior brought his sons to Yankee Stadium, where they began playing catch near the dugout before a game. Junior, 13, and Craig, 12, were among more than a dozen players' children

5

who were horsing around at the time. But for some reason, Martin singled out Ken and Craig for their behavior. The manager told the Yankees' clubhouse attendant to relay a message to Ken Sr. that he had to remove his kids from the clubhouse area as soon as he finished taking batting practice. Other kids could stay, but Ken and Craig had to go. "Why me?" Junior wondered. Martin later explained: "Son, this is work. It's a place for big leaguers, or at least people who act like big leaguers."

The remark bothered both Senior, who never spoke much to his manager after the incident, and Junior, who used to love going to Riverfront Stadium. He vowed never to go back to Yankee Stadium until he really did make the major leagues.

Junior blossomed into a star athlete at Moeller High School in Cincinnati, where he hit over .400 all four years. Scott Schaffner, Moeller's third baseman, once told *Sports Illustrated*, "There were times when he'd hit a ball so far, it was like a golf ball. We played on a field with no fence. You'd see outfielders 500 feet back, and he'd still pop it over their heads."

As a 16-year-old playing for the Midland Cardinals against 18-year-olds in the Connie Mack league World Series, Ken homered three times in the series, once to left field, another to straightaway center and then a rope over the fence in right.

On the football field, Ken was such a superb wide receiver that Schaffner, who was also the school's quarterback, made a habit of throwing the ball over Ken's shoulders and watching the speedy wide receiver pull the pigskin down in full stride. "He could have been just as good at football as he is at baseball," Schaffner insisted. "He was that good."

Ken was equally adept at catching baseballs that were hit over his shoulders. It was his favorite type of catch to make, just as it had been when his brother Craig threw to him on the Riverfront Stadium astroturf. "People always ask why I play such a shallow center field," Ken says. "It's because I wanted to run 'em down like my dad."

Since Junior stayed behind in Cincinnati during the school year while Senior played in New York, they rarely had a chance to see each other play in person. Ken liked the idea of having his dad there to watch him play, but it also made him tense, because he sometimes tried too hard to impress his dad. Senior often encouraged Junior to live up to his own expectations, rather than trying to impress other people — especially his own father, who wanted him to have fun with baseball — but Junior still pressed. Ken's parents were both watching him at Moeller High one day when he struck out twice in successive at bats. "He'd better cut down on his swing," Ken Sr. told his wife. "I think he's trying to leave Earth right now."

One afternoon when the Yankees had an off day in Chicago, Senior planned to fly home to watch Junior play in a big game. Ken had to ask his dad not to come. "He could play under the pressure of scouts watching him, his mother watching him, none of that ever bothered him," said Mike Cameron, Junior's coach at Moeller. "But not his father. Ken Sr. would show up and I'd give him a look, and he'd say, 'I know. I know.'"

As much as Ken's parents supported his athletic interests, they were just as insistent that he behave. Whenever Ken traveled, he always had to call home, even if that meant waking his parents at odd hours of the night. His mother also warned him not to hang out with the wrong crowd. If Ken learned that a friend was doing drugs, she said, he either had to stop seeing that friend immediately or move out of the house.

# 3

# Senior

KEN ADMIRED HIS father, not because he was a celebrity, but because of all the work he had put in to get where he was. Ken Sr. had grown up in such poverty-stricken circumstances that he had to go out and work as a teenager to help his family survive. But that didn't stop Ken from being a three sport star in high school, even though he had to walk five miles to get to the nearest baseball field. Other kids could ride the bus, but Senior saved the $65.10 he received every other week from his job with the Youth Corps and walked the ten mile round trip in shoes patched with cardboard.

The Griffeys lived in a housing project in Donora, Pennsylvania, where Ken Sr.'s mother raised her five children on skimpy welfare checks. The father, a schoolboy teammate of Hall-of-Famer Stan Musial, had left when Ken Sr. was two. When people asked him if he felt that he spoiled his own children, Senior would say, "As much as I could. Don't get me wrong; we always stressed the value of hard work. It's just that I grew up wanting. I didn't want that for my kids."

In Ken Sr.'s class was a girl named Alberta. People called her Birdie. She was a tall, athletic basketball and volleyball player, whose best friend had a crush on Ken. The friend, who was too shy to ask Ken to go out on a date, instead convinced Birdie to ask for her. "No," he told Birdie, "but I'll go out with you instead."

The relationship developed so smoothly that shortly after high school graduation, Ken and Birdie got married. That summer, Ken, who was actually more accomplished in track and football than he was in baseball, was chosen in the 29th round of the 1969 Amateur Draft by the Cincinnati Reds. After the wedding, Ken headed for his assignment with the Reds' minor league farm system. He struggled for the first year and needed to take odd jobs in Donora during the off-season. When Birdie became pregnant, the financial situation became even tougher, and the family had to go on welfare until the season started.

Once Ken Jr. was born, his father began moving up the Reds' minor league ladder. He was just about to get the call to join Cincinnati, when Birdie called him on the phone to tell him that something amazing had happened to seven-month-old Junior. "He walked," she said. "Really, on his own. I didn't hold him or anything. He just started walking."

It wouldn't be the last time Junior was ahead of the game.

# 4

# Minor Adjustments

BECAUSE THE SEATTLE Mariners had baseball's worst record in 1986, they were allowed to make the first selection in the 1987 Amateur Draft. Since the club's inception in 1977, Seattle had never finished with a winning record. But the Mariners' ineptness earned them a million-dollar catch, the very player the team had needed desperately for more than a decade. "He has speed, power, and a good arm," Roger Jongewaard, the Mariners' director of scouting, said of Ken at the time. "He simply has the best overall potential of anyone eligible for the draft."

Over a three-day period, the 26 major-league clubs selected a record 1,263 players in 75 rounds, but the Mariners never hesitated in snatching Ken — nor in signing him. Twenty minutes after being selected, Ken signed his first professional contract with Seattle.

Jongewaard added that the player whom Junior most resembled was Darryl Strawberry, who was then an all-star outfielder for the New York Mets. "Kenny's strong and similar to Darryl in that he's tall with a quick and powerful stroke. Defensively, Darryl's more of a glider in the outfield, although Kenny is quicker and covers more ground. With his gifts — and his family tree doesn't hurt — Kenny could be an all-star regular as well."

Ken worked out with the Mariners for three days in Seattle, meeting many of his future teammates and taking in some games in the Kingdome, Seattle's huge indoor home park. As Ken left for the Mariners' rookie league team in Bellingham, Washington, Mariners fans were all abuzz about the player who figured to be the franchise's first real superstar some day. Jongewaard, though, reminded people in Seattle that "he's going to take a few years to get back here. Remember he's a kid, and we're not going to rush him."

Junior, though, had a different timetable in mind. He thought in the back of his mind that he might one day play in the majors before age forced his father into retirement. Maybe they could even play in same outfield.

Ken became a popular figure in Bellingham, whose 46,000 inhabitants all seemed to love baseball. When he came to bat, the public address announcer would say, "Yes indeedy, what time is it?" to which the crowd would respond: "It's Griffey time."

Ken made it all look easy at the beginning, homering in his first game and finishing his first week as a pro with three homers, eight RBIs, and three stolen bases. He was named the league's Player of the Week for that effort, but then seemed to grow complacent. Things didn't come as easily for Ken as they had in high school, where he could let his talent do all the work. At Bellingham, sometimes lazy mistakes made him look bad. After Ken was picked off at first base, his manager, Rick Sweet, laid it on the line: "Kenny can't be a spectator out there. If he wants to be great, he can't rely on talent; he has to play like a player who's looking for an edge."

Ken had sufficient motivation to progress to major league heights, but he could also find secondary incentives during minor league travel. His first road trip was a ten-hour, all-night ride aboard a 1958 bus that had no bathroom facilities. Ken had to climb into the overhead luggage compartment to stretch out and go to sleep.

Ken had been used to hanging out with his dad, who either took team charter flights or sat in a plane's first class section on every trip. But as Ken's batting average began sinking, so did his spirits. He started to miss his home life just as any other 17-year-old would. His parents had always told him to call if he ever had any questions or just wanted to talk, and one day, Ken called his mom asking for help. She flew in the next day, but instead of giving her son the expected pat on the back, she gave him some stern words about self-discipline, responsibility, and growing up. Ken took the advice to heart and his attitude improved. His average zoomed from .230 to .330 by season's end. His phone bill kept increasing, too, but by then the calls were about the success he was enjoying.

Junior started the 1988 season with San Bernardino in the California League, where he hit .338, while whacking 11 homers and knocking in 42 runs in 58 games. After a back injury sidelined him for two weeks, he moved up to Double-A Vermont. He finished the season as a designated hitter in the Eastern League, and hit .444 during the playoffs. When his father came to watch, reporters asked both Kens to compare themselves. "We do basically everything the same," Junior said. "We run, hit, and throw about the same."

But Senior said that he felt his son could turn out to be the better player: "To me, he's got more power than I will ever have. He's a lot better than I was at the same age."

Junior's rapid development and skyrocketing potential caused such a ripple of excitement that Birdie Griffey began to notice an important shift in fans' attention: "People used to come up to me in the store and say, 'Hey, you're Ken Griffey's wife.' Now they come up and say, 'Hey, you're Ken Griffey's mother.'"

# 5

# Major Story

ALTHOUGH KEN WAS invited to spring training with the Mariners in 1989, everyone connected with the team expected that he would be returned to the minors before the regular season began. "I want him to be there for 20 years," said Jim Lefebvre, Seattle's manager at the time. "If we rush him, it could set him back a couple of years." But Ken moved up the timetable by tearing up the Grapefruit League. In 26 exhibition games, he hit .359 with 33 hits and 21 RBIs.

Lefebvre had been adamant about letting Ken develop his skills in the minors for another season. But Junior's performance and maturity convinced Lefebvre that he wasn't dealing with an ordinary 19-year-old. He had been around major league dugouts and knew what it took to be a major leaguer on and off the field. "This is my 12th training camp," he told people. "That's ten with my dad and two on my own."

Lefebvre called Junior into his office on the final day of roster cuts. "Ken, we know you've had an incredible spring," he began, leading Junior to think he was headed back down again, "so we've decided to make you our center fielder."

Ken couldn't believe it. "Excuse me, I have to use the phone," he said. This was no call for help; it was a call to celebrate.

Ken's arrival was the most anticipated event in the Mariners' brief, 13-year history. "Halley's Comet didn't get this much advance publicity," wrote Bob Finnigan of the *Seattle Times*.

At first Ken looked as though he would pick up where he left off in spring training. In his first major league at bat, he lined a double off Oakland's tough veteran Dave Stewart at the Oakland Coliseum. "The Start of Something Great," the *Seattle*

*Times* proclaimed in a headline — as if there wasn't enough pressure on the teenager. "We've just watched the living definition of the word Impact," Lefebvre added.

But then Junior learned the meaning of the word slump, when he failed to get a hit in his next 18 at bats. Despite the ominous start, the fans in Seattle still anxiously waited for Ken to make his first appearance at the Kingdome. In their 12 previous seasons, Mariners' fans had never had the opportunity to root for a player with Ken's superstar potential.

So when the White Sox came to town for Seattle's home opener, it was no surprise to see a sign in the center field stands that read, "Welcome, King Kenny." People were still settling into their seats after giving Ken a standing ovation in the bottom of the first inning when he swung at Eric King's first pitch. The ball seemed to rocket off Ken's bat so fast that some fans didn't even have time to break the rhythm of their cheer as they watched the ball sail over the fence for Ken's first major league home run.

During that first homestand, Ken set club records by pounding out eight straight hits over three games and by reaching base safely 11 straight times. Joked Finnigan, "He supplied everything but the partridge in a pear tree."

As usual, the Mariners struggled throughout Ken's first season, finishing in sixth place with a 79–83 record. From a personal standpoint, however, Ken's rookie year seemed like a collection of highlight-film dramatics, until an injury cut short his output.

On May 26, Junior hit his first inside-the-park homer against the Yankee team whose manager once told him he couldn't act like a major leaguer. A week later he had his first two-homer game, once again victimizing the Yankees.

On June 4, the Mariners held a Ken Griffey Jr. poster day and the honored star hit another game-winning homer against knuckleball pitcher Charlie Hough. It was the first time in his life that Ken had ever seen a knuckleball. "I don't think anybody's ever been that good at that age," said Mariners' hitting instructor Gene Clines. "He's in his own category. He is a natural."

Yet as striking as Griffey could be with his bat, he could be equally flashy with his glove and rifle-like throwing arm. In Boston, he stunned Red Sox players and fans with dynamic grabs on successive days. First he threw himself high against Fenway Park's Green Monster, the 37-foot-tall fence in left-center field, to snatch an extra base hit away from former AL batting champ Wade Boggs.

The next day, Ken proved that the catch against Boggs wasn't a fluke when he made virtually the same play to rob Tom Brunansky of an extra-base hit.

When the Brewers came to Seattle, Ken made what Lefebvre called "the greatest throw I've ever seen; in fact, the greatest throw I've ever heard about." Brewer all-star Robin Yount hit a ball into the right-center field gap, where it short-hopped the fence. Ken raced to the wall, played the carom perfectly, and fired a strike on the fly to cut down Yount at third base.

Everything was sailing along for Ken, who was leading all rookies in batting average, homers, and RBIs, until a freak accident occurred on July 25. Getting out of the shower of his hotel room, Ken slipped, fell against the tub, and broke a finger on his right hand. The injury caused him to miss the next month of the season, and when he returned to the lineup, he still couldn't grip his bat properly. He managed to hit just .216 with only three homers in the last month of the season. "It was embarrassing," Ken recalls. "You expect to get hurt diving or crashing into a fence. I was just a klutz."

Despite the injury-caused slump, Ken was so popular in Seattle that a local trading card manufacturer produced a Ken

Griffey Jr. chocolate card and sold 800,000 of them. "I had no idea the demand would be this phenomenal," said Mike Cramer, the manufacturer, whose supply couldn't keep up with the demand. "This has gotten out of hand."

Even Ken's newfound celebrity couldn't change the fact that he was still a 19-year-old who needed parental support and direction. In some ways, he was like a normal teenager away at college. When Ken first arrived in Seattle, his mother chose an apartment for him. Since the Mariners weren't allowed to wear jeans or sneakers on road trips, Ken's mom also bought him a suit, tie, and shoes, hoping they'd fit properly. Everyone knew who he was, but Ken still tried to be a normal teenager.

# 6

# Catching On

KEN KNEW THAT there was still a lot of room for improvement in 1990 and he also wanted to live up to the raves from his teammates, who took to calling him "Kid." "This kid is a natural," Mariners' catcher Scott Bradley said. "Guys like Wayne Gretzky, Magic Johnson, and Larry Bird play the game in slow motion. The Kid is like that.

"Every game you know you're going to see something you'll have trouble believing. He never ceases to amaze me. He makes what we call 'you-gotta-be-kidding-me catches' all the time."

In an early season game against the Athletics, Ken brought Bradley's words to light. Oakland's Rickey Henderson hit a soaring fly ball well over Griffey's head. As if he had eyes in the back of his baseball cap, Ken sped towards the fence and threw his arms in front of him just as the ball passed over his shoulder. He snatched the ball out of the air, bounced off the fence, and fired the ball back to the infield, as an astonished Oakland baserunner scrambled back to first base.

The play reminded many people of the famous catch Willie Mays made in the 1954 World Series, when the future Hall-of-Famer reached over his shoulder in full stride to snare a tremendous drive off the bat of Vic Wertz.

In the eyes of many baseball experts, Mays had been the most complete player ever to play the game. By "complete," people meant that he could do everything extraordinarily well. He possessed the rare combination of being able to run, throw, field, hit for average, and hit for power as well as anybody in baseball. Ken had some of Mays's flair. He wore the same number 24 and he displayed some of the same joy for the game that made Mays such a beloved player. "That's a lot of pressure," Lefebvre said of the comparison, "but you can't help but think of Mays when you watch Kenny play every day."

Ken was hardly finished with his Willie Mays imitation. He saved some of his most dazzling displays for Yankee Stadium, a few miles away from where Mays had patrolled center field for the New York Giants when they played at the Polo Grounds.

On April 25, Ken preserved a 2–1 Mariners' lead in the fifth inning by diving to his left to make a backhand grab in the right-center field gap. After sliding on his stomach with the ball in his glove, Ken leapt to his feet, which were still skidding on the wet grass, and fired a strike to first base to double off Steve Sax, who bounced his helmet against the ground in disbelief. "Every time he makes one of those plays, you think, 'He'll never top that one,' " Lefebvre said.

The very next night the Mariners beat the Yanks, 6–2 and Ken again brought the fans to their feet with a spectacular fourth-inning grab that robbed Jesse Barfield of what would have been his 200th career homer.

Barfield ripped a shot towards the left-center field power alley, which is deeper in Yankee Stadium than in most parks. As soon as Ken heard the contact, he bolted after the ball from his normal shallow position, reached the warning track at full speed and, after feeling the grass under his feet turn to dirt, leapt up without ever looking at the eight-foot-tall fence. Several Mariner pitchers, who were sitting in the bullpen directly behind the spot where the ball was headed, saw an arm fling over the fence and whip back in the other direction like a lightning-fast slingshot. The ball just disappeared. Ken had snared it.

"I wasn't mad," Barfield said later in utter astonishment. "I was waiting for someone to pinch me."

20

Ken Jr. wasn't the only happy Griffey that night. As the standing ovation for the Junior was just starting to hush, Ken Sr., who had recently retired from the Reds, was still yelling and pumping his fist in a seat behind home plate.

In the sixth inning, Barfield ripped a shot to right center. Again Ken took off after the ball. Barfield normally watches his fly balls sail out of the park just as most sluggers do, but this time he glanced at the ground, afraid to see another would-be dinger disappear into Junior's glove. This time, the ball landed seven rows into the bleachers, too deep even for Ken to snare. When Barfield reached home plate, he was greeted by happy teammates, ready to congratulate him on whacking his 200th dinger. But before acknowledging his teammates, Barfield turned to Mariners' catcher Scott Bradley and said, "If he had caught that one, I was going to retire."

After the game, reporters were asking Senior about his son's catch. "I'm in awe the same as you guys are," he said. "Yes, I'm a very proud dad."

The catch called to mind a similar play that Senior had made in 1985 when he was with the Yanks. Boston's Marty Barrett had hit a fly ball towards the left field line. Unlike the deep alleys at Yankee Stadium, the fences along the lines at Fenway Park are very close, with fans able to reach over the fence and interfere with balls that would normally hit the top of the wall. Still, on that day, Senior was able to leap over the fence and make the grab as his glove hit the arms of fans who were hungry for a souvenir. Senior jokingly compared the two catches this way: "Well, you know Kenny didn't have to fight off anybody when he made *his* catch. But seriously, what amazes me is that I might have made two or three of those in almost 20 years of playing ball. Look at him, he makes them all the time, like there's a rocket on his feet and a magnet in his glove."

Fans loved Ken's acrobatics, and voted him in as the starting American League center fielder in the 1990 All-Star Game. Senior was in the stands again when Junior, still just 20, became the second-youngest starter in All-Star history.

# 7

# All in the Family

WATCHING HIS SON shine left Ken Sr. with one final baseball wish: he wanted to play in the same outfield as his son. The Mariners had talked about offering a contract to Senior for the rest of the 1990 season. And on August 31, the family's dream came true. Before 27,000 fans at the Kingdome, Ken Sr. played left field and batted second in the Seattle lineup, while Junior played center and batted third. "I was so nervous, it was like being a rookie again," 40-year-old Senior said. "Of all the things that have happened to me — the World Series, the All-Star games, everything — this is number one. This is the best thing that's ever happened to me."

Junior was just as elated, knowing that his rapid ascent to the majors had helped fulfill his father's wish. "Dad's given me everything kids dream about," said Ken, who asked for the words "The Kid" to be inscribed on his new bats. "This is the one thing I could give him."

Before the game, the two Griffeys joked about playing together as pros for the first time.

"What happens if I call you off a ball?" Junior asked.

"With my legs? You better," Senior answered. "If you don't, you're grounded, and I'm taking your car away."

The two began the family celebration in the first inning, as they bounced back-to-back singles through the infield, and later came in to score the Mariners' first two runs of the game.

In the Royals' half of the sixth, KC's Bo Jackson ripped a shot off the left field wall. The carom bounced back to Senior, who threw a one-hop strike to nail the fleet-footed Jackson at second base. After the play, Senior looked over at Junior, who shouted, "You're learning. Guess it runs in the family." Later, Junior told reporters, "It seemed like a father-son game, like we were out playing catch in the backyard."

Even Jackson was impressed. "I didn't expect that old guy to throw me out," he said. "I'd have been mad if anyone else had done that, but it was a nice piece of history."

There was more history to come. On September 14, Senior and Junior hit back-to-back homers against Kirk McKaskill of the California Angels. "It's like everything we do is a first," said Senior, who would hit only one more homer, his 152nd, in his extended career.

Ken finished the season with a .300 batting average, a plateau he has surpassed every year since. He also won his first Gold Glove Award for outstanding defensive play, starting another streak that still has no end in sight.

# 8

# Sticks and Stones

KEN'S SUPERSTAR ABILITY and easygoing nature were quickly turning him into the game's most popular player and therefore a fine ambassador for baseball. Before the 1991 season began, Ken led a group of major league all-stars on a tour of Japan, and was selected as the MVP of their exhibition series. His playful nature also made him a hit with the fans who, before long, were chanting "Junior, Junior" in both English and Japanese.

Back home, North American fans made him the American League's top vote-getter for the 1991 All-Star Game with 2.2 million votes. He appeared on talk shows and was one of the first players asked by Major League Baseball to do publicity for their Stay in School program for youngsters.

However, as beloved as Ken had become and as used to reporters as he had been from a young age, he was particularly hurt by an article written by Steve Kelley of the *Seattle Times* during the All-Star break. The article, written in the form of a letter to Ken, questioned his drive and motivation, and asked him, point-blank, if he was prepared to make the jump from being a very good player to becoming a superstar or whether he was a player who would never quite give everything he had on the field.

Griffey didn't feel the column was fair and called Kelley to clear the air about how much baseball meant to him. Fair or not, the article motivated Ken so much, Lefebvre later said, "it set him on fire."

In the next month, Ken hit .418 with eight homers and 34 RBIs, league-leading marks in all three categories. "It was a bad article," Ken said later, "but it came out good because it made me think about the person I want to be and what I can accomplish in this game."

Former Mariners' right fielder Jeff Leonard said he noticed an immediate difference in Ken's approach to playing the outfield. The previous year, Leonard said, Griffey would walk over during a pitching change and want to talk about "rap and rock bands. This year all he talks about is baseball. He asks about the cutoff man, whether so-and-so hits the ball the other way, that kind of thing."

Soon after the article, Ken appropriately hit his first career grand slam at Yankee Stadium.

In another game against the Baltimore Orioles, Ken reached over the fence to rob Randy Milligan of a grand slam in the top half of an inning and then hit his own grand slam in the bottom half — an eight-run swing by one player in one inning.

Ken finished the year with 22 homers, 100 RBIs, and a .327 average, which made him the first player in either league to improve his average by at least 25 points in his second and third seasons since 1974 and 1975 when two players turned the trick. One was perennial all-star George Brett. The other was Ken Griffey Sr.

But more important to Ken, the Mariners had finally finished above .500 for the first time in their history. Their 83–79 record was only good enough for fifth place in the tough AL West, but at least it was a move in the right direction.

# 9

# Star of Stars

KEN WAS FAST becoming a fixture in the Seattle community for his exploits on and off the field. When Gordon Lakey, a scout for the Toronto Blue Jays, was in town during the 1992 season to watch Griffey, a reporter asked him just how good The Kid was. "Let me tell you," Lakey began. "You don't have enough paper. Let me put it this way: I have not seen him unable to do anything on the baseball field. He does what he wishes."

The Seattle community was also becoming increasingly grateful to Ken for the times he performed great deeds without even picking up a bat. The Make-A-Wish Foundation is an organization that grants wishes to children facing life-threatening illnesses. For many of these kids, especially those in the Seattle area, their big request is a chance to meet Ken, and he has welcomed dozens onto the field at the Kingdome and other ballparks since he first met a child through the program in 1989, when he was just 19 himself.

In helping fulfill a typical wish, the Mariners provide the youngster with box seats to a game at the Kingdome. Ken meets the child before batting practice and brings him or her onto the field and into the dugout for a 45-minute chat about striving in life and not giving up the fight against a particular illness. Since many of the kids are often Ken's most knowledgeable fans, they ask good questions about his early life in the minor leagues and what it's finally like to play in the majors. Then if the kids are up to it, Ken has a catch with them.

After tossing a ball back and forth with one wide-eyed nine-year-old named Keith, Ken brought the youngster into the Mariners' locker room, signed one of his own shirts; and gave it to the boy.

Ken's popularity and great play landed him a starting spot in the American League's starting lineup in the 1992 All-Star Game at San Diego's Jack Murphy Stadium. Ken batted seventh in the Americans' lineup, which ironically was one spot behind Baltimore's Cal Ripken Jr. and one spot ahead of Sandy Alomar Jr. Like Ken, both players had fathers with the same first name who preceeded them as major leaguers.

In the first inning, Ken stroked an opposite-field single against Atlanta lefty Tom Glavine, the NL's reigning Cy Young Award winner, whom the Americans touched up for four first-inning runs.

Two innings later, Ken faced Chicago Cubs righty Greg Maddux, who would go on to win the NL's Cy Young Award in each of the next three seasons, the next two with Atlanta. Ken worked the count to 2–0, and then lashed an outside pitch over the left field fence. As soon as he reached the American League dugout, Ken thought back to the 1980 All-Star Game in Los Angeles. "Just like my dad," he told his AL teammates. "Who'd he hit it against?" Minnesota's Kirby Puckett wanted to know. "Tommy John," Ken answered. "Did he win MVP?" Alomar asked. "Yup," Ken said proudly.

In his last at bat, Ken led off a four-run sixth with a double to right. The American Leaguers won the game, 13–6, and Ken won the MVP award a dozen years after his father had won his. "I'm just lucky I got three hits," Ken said afterwards. "First thing I'm going to do is call my dad and tell him 'We're even.' "

But in terms of team accomplishments, Junior was a long way from being even with his dad. Junior's personal numbers were as good as ever in 1992. He hit .323 and finished with what were at the time career highs in homers (27) and RBIs (103). But under new manager Bill Plummer, the Mariners plummeted to a dismal 64–98 record, their worst since Junior's arrival. Junior wouldn't say so publicly yet, but his frustration with losing was simmering.

# 10

# The Streak

WINNING THE ALL-Star MVP award had helped push Ken further up the list of the game's elite players. "He's the man in center field now," said Minnesota's Kirby Puckett, an eight-time all-star center fielder who played on two World Series winners with the Twins. "He does it all better than anybody."

At the time Junior was also being compared to Barry Bonds, the left fielder who won back-to-back MVP honors with the Pittsburgh Pirates in 1990 and 1991 and would be heading for another as a member of the San Francisco Giants in 1993. Like Junior, Barry was raised by a baseball dad — Bobby, who played for eight major league teams in 12 seasons. And like Junior, Barry Bonds is an all-around force with speed, power, and a knack for flashing leather in the outfield. "The only difference between Junior and Barry is that Bonds is a little older and more mature and has been in pennant races," said Lou Piniella, who took over as the Mariners' manager in 1993. "Junior is very, very talented. Hopefully we'll get him to that point in the next year or two."

There has also been an obvious difference the contrasting perceptions of Junior as fun-loving and of Bonds as aloof, uncooperative, and moody. "I really think Barry has gotten a bad rap," Senior insisted. "He's not a bad guy. He and Junior are both talented, but they're both very different people."

They also played in different situations. Bonds was heading from the Pirates, who had won three straight divisional crowns, to the Giants, who were also a solid team in the NL West; Ken was playing for his third manager in three seasons, as Lou Piniella replaced the fired Plummer in the off-season.

Ken had dazzled so many fans with his speed and defense that his hitting could, at times, be overlooked. Even Piniella downplayed Ken's longball skills when he said, "He isn't really a home run hitter. He's just a tremendous all-around hitter who happens to hit a lot of homers because he hits a lot of balls hard."

Ken started hitting big-league homers so consistently at such a young age, people may have lost track of the fact that only five players in history had reached the 100 home run mark faster than he had. Junior's single-season homer totals were fairly consistent for the first four seasons: 16, 22, 22, and 27. But he started bombing away in bunches right around the 1993 All-Star break.

Ken didn't win the MVP Award that time, but on the day before the game, he helped the American League win a home run hitting contest by whacking a batting-practice pitch off the warehouse beyond the right field fence, 500 feet from home plate in Baltimore's two-year-old Camden Yards. It was the first time a player had ever hit the warehouse.

Then later in the season, Ken began his assault on what people in Seattle remember simply as The Streak. It began innocently enough when Ken homered at — where else? — Yankee Stadium against New York's Paul Gibson. The next night he smacked another against the Yankees' ace southpaw Jimmy Key. Ken then homered in each game of the Mariners' four-game series in Cleveland, and people were searching for the record books. In major league history, only Dale Long of the Pirates and Don Mattingly of the Yankees, who had each hit home runs in eight straight ballgames, had ever homered in more consecutive contests.

When the Mariners returned home, the fans began waving banners urging Ken to go after the record. "Lucky 7," one sign said. "Seventh Heaven," read another. And in his second at bat,

Ken crunched a grand slam against Minnesota's Kevin Tapani.

The next night the signs were out in force again. "Junior's Crazy 8," said one. In center field was another saying "He Eight the Whole Thing." This was Ken's chance to tie the record.

In the first inning, with the crowd standing throughout the at bat, he struck out against Minnesota's Willie Banks. Then in the fourth, he grounded out to first. In the seventh he came up for the third time against Banks, who was tossing a masterful one-hit shutout at the time. Banks stared in for the sign from his catcher, who called for a fastball. As soon as he threw it, Banks said later, he figured Griffey would hit it out. "It wasn't the pitch," Banks said. "I threw it on the outside corner. He just had that look in his eye." With one swing, Ken etched his name in history, driving a towering blast off the facade of the Kingdome's third deck.

When he reached home plate, Ken could barely find the base through the swarm of hugging teammates. The Twins were winning the game, 4–1, but the score hardly mattered to the fans, whose boisterous cheers brought Ken back out of the dugout twice for rare tips of the cap. Even after two pitches to Jay Buhner, Seattle's next hitter, home plate umpire Drew Scott had to stop the game so the noise would die down.

When Ken ran back out to center field for the next inning, the crowd gave him another standing ovation. He was one game away from having the record all to himself.

More than 30,000 fans bought tickets on the day of Seattle's next game. The fans, hoping for history, had one more banner to wave: "Junior's Nine Lives."

Against Scott Erickson and Larry Casian, Ken had a scream-ing single and a scorching double to show for his first three at bats. In the seventh, Casian hung a slow curveball up in the strike zone, the kind of pitch Ken has hit out of many parks. This time he popped it up. The streak was over. "If he had hit another one," Mariners' pitcher Erik Hanson said, "the roof would have come off, and we'd have an outdoor stadium. That's how loud the place was getting."

Ken finished the season with 45 home runs, but said his biggest thrill was the off-season birth of his son, Trey Kenneth Griffey. Instead of a congratulatory note, the Mariners sent a signed contract in Trey's name for the year 2012. "His agent says they didn't offer enough money," Ken joked at the time. "I'm his agent."

The Mariners' fourth-place finish, however, didn't leave Junior in a joking mood. At 82–80, they were over .500 for only the second time in franchise history, but they also finished 12 games out of first place and were seemingly getting no closer.

# 11

# Striking Possibilities

KEN FELT HE couldn't keep quiet about his team's poor showing any longer. During the off-season, Junior was taking some good-natured ribbing from Senior, who was showing off his World Series rings. "You don't have any of these, do you?" Senior said.

The remark bothered Junior, who spoke up about his discontent over management's inability to improve the team. He was a superstar, but in five years he had never been in a pennant race with the Mariners. Piniella backed Junior's remarks, saying he, too, was upset at the team's woes, and the franchise was in turmoil.

Ken played a role in another controversy when Yankee manager Buck Showalter said he was bothered by some of the habits Ken maintained since the days when his baseball outfits were too big for him. Before a game in Seattle, Showalter told reporters: "I shouldn't say this publicly, but a guy like Ken Griffey Jr., the game's boring to him. He comes on the field and his hat's on backward, and his shirttail's hanging out . . . . To me, that's lack of respect for the game."

Ken explained that he had to wear his outfits like that when he was a boy. "Buck doesn't know me," he said. "He doesn't know what I'm about. He doesn't know that when I wore those things like that, people said I looked cute. So I got used to it. As far as fun, as far as respect for the game, show me one player out here having as much fun as I do. I love baseball. Shoot, if I couldn't play in the Kingdome, I'd be playing softball in the park. You don't have to pay me; just give me a bat and a ball."

Despite what Showalter might have thought, the fans took to

Junior in increasing numbers. Ken received a record 6 million votes in the 1994 All-Star balloting. That shattered the previous record set by Minnesota's Rod Carew, who received 4.2 million in 1977, the year he almost hit .400.

Ken's love of the game's challenge was never more evident than at the 1994 All-Star Game in Pittsburgh. Once again, the Home Run Derby the day before the actual game was Ken's show. He cranked seven homers, including five shots into the upper deck, in leading the American League to a 17–11 victory against the Nationals. In the 25 years since Three Rivers Stadium had been built, only 11 balls had been hit into the upper deck in actual games.

Ken was still in a playful mood after All-Star batting practice, when a reporter asked him if there was anything his manager Lou Piniella hadn't seen him do. Ken gave it a thought and, keeping a straight face, told the man, "Lou won't let me hit right-handed. I've been asking him. I tell him it'll round out my game. He says no, and I'm upset about it."

Most reporters knew not to take Ken seriously, but when one man started skipping down the hallway that led to the press room figuring he had a good story, Ken had to chase him down and tell him he was only kidding. Despite Ken's displeasure with the Mariners' losing, Claire Smith of *The New York Times* later described Junior's daily approach to baseball very simply: "While others were merely holding down major league jobs, he was doing something a lot more lofty and fulfilling — playing a game."

He played it better than ever in 1994 and for a while was on a pace to break Roger Maris's 23-year-old record for home runs in a season of 61. First Ken broke Mickey Mantle's record for homers in the season's first two months. And when he hit his 31st homer on June 21, he broke Babe Ruth's mark of 30 HRs before July 1. Junior seemed to be sending a message that we haven't seen anything yet.

"He's so good at it," marveled Mariners' right fielder Jay Buhner, "it gets a little irritating. Like it's so effortless. I think, 'Is it that easy, man? Is it *that* easy?'"

Ken, continuing to play smash ball, had a league-leading 40 home runs and was in hot pursuit of Maris's single-season mark when a labor dispute put an end to the 1994 season on August 12. Ken, who totally supported the player's strike, just shrugged off his missed opportunity to chase one of baseball's most cherished records. "I was still 21 away. It wasn't like I was close. I was close, but I wasn't so close. It is disappointing, but it wasn't like I tasted it. It wasn't like I had 58 with a week and a half to play. We had six weeks to go, and I still had to hit 21 just to tie Maris."

What really disturbed Ken was that the Mariners were finally in the midst of mounting a charge at a division championship, and that the excellent play of a great number of players was making 1994 one of the most exciting seasons in memory.

"I'm really frustrated because it was a good year for baseball to break through as far as the records changing," Griffey said. "We had Frank Thomas going for the Triple Crown, and Albert Belle was trying to do it, too. I would have tried my best to hold them off. Everyone was interested in baseball. Everyone wanted to see what was going to happen. Everyone wanted the whole year."

The extended off-season did provide some positive benefits for Ken, though. He got more time to spend with his wife, Melissa, and his son, Trey. "I'm on baby-sitting patrol," smiled Ken. Ken has also become partners with other sports superstars, including Joe Montana, Shaquille O'Neal, Wayne Gretzky, and Andre Agassi, in a chain of sports restaurants called All-Star Cafe.

But as much as Ken is enjoying himself in the off-season, he's hoping that the labor dispute is quickly settled. Because Ken can't wait to get to spring training and to start another season.

And soon Ken may have another Griffey to help him propel the Mariners to the top of the AL West. Ken's brother Craig spent the 1994 season at the Mariners' Double-A affiliate in Jacksonville, Florida. But with or without his brother, Ken is ready to continue both his claim as the best all-around player in baseball and his assault on the major league record books.

"I think my concentration is better than it's ever been," Ken said after the season. "I'm still learning and I've dedicated myself to being as good as I can be. So watch out, I'll be back next year just having fun playing ball." And as Ken's agent, Rick Licht, pointed out, "He's only 24, and he believes in his talent. Maybe last season was just a warmup for the real thing."

# PHOTO SECTION

Happy in Seattle.
Courtesy of Seattle Mariners.

Home run.
Courtesy of Seattle Mariners.

Father and son.
AP/Wide World Photos.

Junior makes a wish come true.
Courtesy of Seattle Mariners.

Spectacular!
AP/Wide World Photos.

A happy Tiger.
Courtesy of Auburn University.

Frank lends a helping hand.
Courtesy of Chicago White Sox.

Frank steps into the pitch.
SPORTSCHROME EAST/WEST Robert Tringalli, Jr.

It's out of here!
Courtesy of Chicago White Sox.

A pair of All-Stars.
Tony Inzerillo.

# FRANK THOMAS

# 1

# Jack of all Sports

FRANK EDWARD THOMAS was born May 27, 1968 in Columbus, Georgia. His mother Charlie Mae was a textile worker, while his father Frank Thomas Sr. held two jobs. First he worked as a bail bondsman for the city of Columbus. But he also spent time as a deacon in the community's Baptist church. Frank Sr. enjoyed both jobs, because they allowed him to spend a lot of time with people who needed good advice and who often looked for help in their lives. And he took great care to expose his children to the idea of helping the community.

As a boy, Frank liked many sports and found that he was good at almost all of them. He played Little League baseball, Pop Warner football, and basketball in the playgrounds around his house. "There was always something special about my son," Frank Sr. has told people. "He had a gift and, most important, he was willing to learn."

When Frank was nine years old, his football coach, Chester Murray, told Frank Sr., "Mr. Thomas, your son will be a professional athlete someday."

"Really," Frank Sr. replied. "In which sport?"

"I don't know," the coach answered. "What does he like to play most? Whatever it is, that's the sport he'll play professionally."

That was in 1977, the year Frank considers the most important in his life. During that year he began to understand that his talent for playing sports was unusually good. But it was also the year he first learned about painful loss. Late that summer, Frank's two-year-old sister Pamela contracted leukemia, a form of cancer. Even though there were seven years in age between them, Frank was the second-youngest in the family of eight, and always assumed it would be his responsibility to take care of baby Pamela. And after being everybody's "little brother" for so long, it was also something he looked forward to. But Pam passed away on Thanksgiving Day, 1977. Frank has two children of his own now, and when he thinks of them, he often thinks of Pamela, and he is always thankful for their health. Frank would face many disappointments in his life, especially those having to do with baseball. But when he did, he could always remember how he dealt with losing Pamela. After Frank dealt with the death of his sister, other setbacks would seem minor by comparison.

As Frank grew older, he became even better at the sports he loved. But it wasn't easy. Frank was the youngest of five brothers who all loved to play sports. Because he was the youngest, Frank always wanted to tag along so that he could hang around the older boys and play in their games around the neighborhood. A lot of times, this meant that he had to carry one of his brothers' equipment or play a position that wasn't his favorite. But he also learned what it took to be just a little bit better at many things by watching his brothers and their friends.

By the time Frank arrived at Columbus High School, he was already showing off his remarkable athletic skills. As a high school basketball player, Frank was a 6-foot, 4-inch muscular power forward who led his team in rebounds and could bury the outside jump shot as well as anybody on his team.

As a football player, he played tight end for Columbus High and earned a reputation as a big player with unusually soft hands for catching and equally big shoulders for blocking. It often took the opposing team two, three, or even four players to tackle Frank once he caught a pass. And when he wasn't blocking or catching balls over the middle, Frank was also the team's place kicker. In his senior season, he converted 15 extra point attempts without a miss.

But as good as Frank was at the other two sports, he was an even better baseball player. In his final three years of high school, Frank batted over .400 and led his team in home runs. Columbus went to the Georgia State championship in each of those years, winning once and losing twice in the final game. In 1986, his senior year, Frank batted a hefty .440, was named high school player of the year for the city of Columbus, and brought droves of professional scouts to the city.

But Frank never got carried away with himself. In fact, what most impressed Bobby Howard, Frank's high school coach, was the way Frank tried not to show off and the way he put winning ahead of his own statistics, even with the scouts watching to see how far the ball would travel off his bat. "He was our leader," Coach Howard remembered. "If we had a big lead, he wanted to see the other guys get in there and play. He was not a know-it-all. In fact he was usually the guy who chalked up the lines on the baseball and football fields. That's not a spoiled kid; that's a serious young man."

He was serious enough about baseball to study statistics about his favorite major leaguers, to read articles and books about hitting, and even to cut out most of the fat from his diet, something that certainly never stopped him from growing to be big and strong. Although he didn't have one particular sports hero, he very much admired Dave Winfield and Dave Parker, two power-hitting outfielders he enjoyed watching on television when he was a teenager.

Frank especially liked Parker and Winfield because they were large men, as he was, and they could hit some tremendous home runs. But unlike a lot of hitters their size, Winfield and Parker both hit for high batting averages. Parker twice won the National League batting title, and Winfield once missed winning the American League crown by less than a point. They were the type of hitter Thomas wanted to be: a slugger who could also hit for a high average and help his team in many ways.

# 2

# Rough Draft

FRANK FELT HE should make a decision about which sport he most wanted to pursue. He consulted with his family and decided that he wanted to play baseball, the sport in which he had made his greatest improvement. In June of 1986, the major league teams held their Amateur Draft to select the top players from high schools and colleges across the country. This was a bit like choosing sides for a game in his neighborhood, except that one of these teams was expected to choose Frank with the hope that he would play in the majors one day. But while teams knew about Frank's baseball ability, they also knew what a good football player he was. Even if they drafted him, the teams realized, Frank still might decide to accept a football scholarship instead.

Some players, such as Bo Jackson and Deion Sanders, have since gone on to play both baseball and football in the pros, but others have had to choose their favorite sport and stick with it. Baseball teams were concerned that if they used one of their draft picks to select Frank, he might decide to play college football instead of baseball. Taking Frank would be a gamble for any team.

So Draft Day turned into a great disappointment for Frank, as round after round of the draft went by, but no team called his name. In three days, the 26 major league teams chose 1,423 players, who they hoped might one day be good enough to play for their clubs. But nobody picked Frank Thomas. His football ability was working against his baseball career. "It wasn't like the scouts didn't even see me," Frank remembered telling his father. "What happened?" Frank was upset. For two days, he didn't want to talk to his parents or see his friends. "If a team had drafted me, I would have signed with them on the spot. That was my dream — to play baseball. I didn't know what to do."

Frank decided to take the negative memories from the draft and turn them into a positive. He was offered a scholarship to play football at Auburn University in Alabama. Auburn Tigers football coach Pat Dye told Frank that he could also play on the baseball team there, even though that meant he would have to skip spring football practice. Frank was determined to work even harder at his baseball, so he could become the kind of player the scouts couldn't possibly ignore the next year . . . or the year after that...or however long it took him to get his chance to show what he could do.

# 3

# Auburn Tiger

AUBURN ALMOST ALWAYS had a highly-ranked, star-studded football team. In 1986, the year before Frank arrived, the Tigers' star running back Bo Jackson won the Heisman Trophy, awarded to the best player in college football. And like Thomas, Jackson was also a star player on the baseball team. The 1987 team was good enough to keep Frank on the bench for most of the year. As the backup tight end, Frank played in parts of eight games and caught only three passes for 45 yards. The Tigers defeated USC that year in the Citrus Bowl and finished sixth in the national polls. Three members of the team, Lawyer Tillman, Anthony Bruce, and Brent Fullwood, went on to careers in the NFL.

Frank hit .359 and broke the school record with 21 home runs, one of which traveled over the center field scoreboard at Georgia Tech Stadium and made the highlight films on many sportscasts throughout the country that evening. A week later, with no television cameras at the game, Frank hit a ball at Mississippi State that sailed over the left field fence, dented a pickup truck, and frightened some students who were starting to cook hot dogs on a barbeque in a nearby yard.

At the end of the season, Frank was named to *Baseball America's* freshman All-America team. Reporters for two sports magazines called him a "sure-fire" major league prospect.

Hal Baird, the Tigers' baseball coach, saw obvious compari-sons between Frank and Jackson, but insisted, "Bo was always a football and baseball player; Frank, I believe, was a baseball player who also played football. Frank understood the art of hitting better than any player I've seen."

After the baseball season ended, Frank dedicated himself to earning more playing time during his sophomore football season. He was always grateful for the lessons that the demanding work of football practice had taught him, even though he didn't get much of a chance to play. "Playing football for Auburn was like a new world for me," Frank has told people. "I learned what hard work means. When I got my chance, 80,000 people wanted to see what I could do."

Frank wanted to do everything a little better. He worked hard at lifting weights and improving his quickness with sprint drills that would allow him to shoot into the holes of the defensive secondary as effectively as some of the Auburn wide receivers. But Coach Dye saw Thomas as a blocking tight end, the type who could open holes for the Auburn running backs. On the first day of practice before his sophomore season, Thomas was setting a block for one of his teammates, who ran up too close to Frank and stepped on the back of his right leg. Frank fell down awkwardly, straining some ligaments in his right knee. He was told he could miss the rest of football season. On top of that, Frank developed bone spurs in his left ankle. He then decided to drop gridirons and concentrate on diamonds.

# 4

# Slugging Sensation

FRANK'S KNEE HEALED in time for his second season of spring baseball, and Coach Baird felt like a lucky man to have Auburn's best hitter back in the lineup. Word spread quickly about Auburn's sophomore slugger, although Frank sometimes found the attention embarrassing. One afternoon, the University of Houston team arrived at Auburn's Plainsman's Park and began doing pre-game stretching exercises near their dugout, while the Tigers were taking batting practice. But when Frank stepped into the batting cage, the Cougar players stopped stretching in order to watch the Big Guy take his swings. Was it true, the visitors wondered, that this player could scorch balls over the 45-foot-high wall beyond the center field fence? Twice that afternoon, Frank showed them that he could by smashing balls high over the wall.

The Houston players couldn't believe it. Apparently, the three men who would pitch for the Cougars that day did believe it, because they walked Frank four times. In his fifth time at bat, Frank hit two long fouls and then, frustrated, swung at a bad pitch for strike three. That particular at bat was a sign of things to come, and Frank would have to learn from it.

In his sophomore season, Frank found that teams had developed a new strategy when he came to the plate. They wouldn't give him anything good to hit. "It was like the playground all over again," his father remembered. "Boys used to throw the ball over the backstop so Frank wouldn't hit it." This was bad enough on the playgrounds or in Little League, but Frank was really getting tired of it in college. He wanted to hit. Even though he didn't mind drawing walks, something his father had always told him was a big help to his team, it was hard for Frank not to swing at those pitches outside of the strike zone, even though he knew better. But Frank's hitting coach at Auburn, Steve Renfro, finally convinced him to maintain his patience at the plate. "Pitchers aren't going to just give you pitches on a silver platter," Renfro said. "You have to make them throw you something good, something *you* want to hit. You have to be patient. A lot of good hitters at your level can swing a bat, but the ones who make an impact in the major leagues are the ones who make the pitcher throw them their pitch."

If Frank started swinging at bad pitches, he would start seeing fewer good ones and eventually lose his command of the strike zone. "I have to make my hitting zone smaller than the strike zone," Frank reminded himself, even though it wasn't easy. Frank hit just nine home runs in his second season at Auburn, but his batting average shot up to .385 and he led the Southeastern Athletic Conference in walks. The Tigers won the first of two successive conference titles, and Thomas began gaining a reputation as a hitter who wouldn't swing at a bad pitch. Although his slugging average (number of total bases divided by official at bats — walks not included) decreased, his on-base average (number of times reaching base divided by total at bats) increased. Although some people felt he should hit the longball better because of his imposing size, Frank was determined to be a complete hitter who could hit for both average and power.

After that second season Frank joined the best college players in the country for the U.S. Olympic Team tryouts. Future major leaguers such as Ben McDonald, Jim Abbott, Ed Sprague, and Scott Servais were among those at the tryout camp in Tennessee. Frank was one of the team's best hitters during its exhibition games, but when it came time to make the final selections for the team, Frank wasn't one of them. Instead Coach Mark Marquess decided to go with another future major leaguer, Tino Martinez, at first base. The Americans won the gold medal without Frank. For the second time in his career, he had suffered a major setback. This one reminded him of the 1986 Draft, when teams weren't willing to take a chance on a first baseman who could also play football.

Frank used the Olympic snub to motivate him and make him an even better player. He topped off his fine collegiate career by hitting .403 while belting 19 home runs, knocking in 83 runs, and being named *Baseball America's* College Player of the Year. Frank, who set the Auburn career record for homers with 49, was so good that Coach Baird ranked him ahead of Bo Jackson. "Frank is the greatest player we've ever had," he insisted.

Some major league teams give players psychological aptitude tests to see how well their minds will react to certain situations that require them to make fast, but smart, decisions. While many teams would not release the results of those tests, a scout for the New York Mets said Frank had scored higher than any amateur player in the country. Other teams gave him similar drills to test his poise, his intelligence, and his ability to work through problems. The Chicago White Sox were one of the teams most interested in Thomas. Larry Himes, the White Sox general manager at the time, figured Frank's talent and maturity would help him get through the minor leagues in a short period of time and eventually help him adjust to the pressures of being in the major leagues, where the pitching is faster, the crowds are bigger, and the expectations are greater.

# 5

# Re-Draft

SURE ENOUGH, THE White Sox, who had the seventh pick in the 1989 Amateur Draft, used it to select Frank. Each big league team has affiliates at different levels of its minor league systems. As is the case with other teams, the White Sox maintained an agreement with affiliates on the beginner (A), intermediate (AA), and advanced (AAA) minor league levels.

Frank was sent to Sarasota, Florida, where two of the White Sox's A teams played. He split his time between those teams, and in 236 at bats during the second half of the 1989 season, he hit .288 with five home runs and 41 RBIs. It was enough to make him believe that he could make the move up to Chicago if he had a good spring training the next year.

In spring training, Frank finally would get to play against major leaguers, the same people he had watched on television and read about in newspapers and magazines back in Columbus. But instead of being in awe of these players, Frank felt he could play with them and against them as well as anyone. That's what he had worked for.

But Frank was in for his third serious baseball disappointment, and it wouldn't have been so bad if he hadn't been so good. In fact, Frank looked like an all-star in spring training, the most dynamic hitter of all the players in the White Sox organization. He hit .500 in 12 exhibition games, and made a lot of people in the ChiSox organization believe that he belonged in Chicago. But Larry Himes, the man who had drafted Frank and called the shots for the White Sox, thought that Frank needed more experience and work on his defense at first base. So Frank started the season at the Double-A level, with the White Sox affiliate in Birmingham, Alabama.

The same day that Frank was told he was going to be sent down, the White Sox were playing an exhibition game against the Texas Rangers and Frank got a chance to bat against Nolan Ryan, one the greatest pitchers in the history of the game. Ryan, whose fastball had once been clocked at 104 miles-per-hour, had struck out more batters than any pitcher in baseball history and had also pitched six no-hitters (he eventually tossed number seven before he retired). No other pitcher has ever hurled more than three no-hitters in his major league career. Frank saw his chance to hit against Ryan as a difficult challenge, but also as a great opportunity. If he could hit against Ryan, he could hit against anybody.

Being patient, Frank took the first pitch for a ball, even though he barely saw it go by. He took another and then fouled off a pitch. The count went to three balls and two strikes. Frank had to make a good decision about the next pitch. He wanted to take a good rip, but he didn't want people to see him lose patience and swing at a pitch out of the strike zone just because he was trying too hard. Ryan stared at his catcher. Then he wound up and zipped Frank a curveball. The pitch had eyes for the outside corner, and Frank knew it would be a strike. He swung just hard enough to make contact, but to his surprise the ball rocketed down the left field line, landing well beyond the fence and surrounding bullpen area. Estimates in local newspapers the next day had the ball traveling between 475 and 500 feet. Frank Thomas, not yet a major league rookie, had blasted a home run against future Hall-of-Famer Nolan Ryan.

Jeff Torborg, the Chicago manager at the time, had seen enough of Frank to believe he should start the season in Chicago. But Himes was sticking to his guns. Ready or not, Frank would travel to Birmingham for more minor league experience before getting his chance in Chicago. Although

Birmingham was a step above where Frank had been the previous year, it wasn't the major leagues. It wasn't the famous Comiskey Park on the South Side of Chicago, home of one of baseball's oldest teams. That's where Frank really wanted to play.

But even though Frank was the rage of spring training, he had to wait. Even though some people predicted that Thomas would be the American League's Rookie of the Year if he had the chance, he was still sent down. When Carlton Fisk, Chicago's veteran catcher, was asked if he thought Frank could stand up to the American League pitching someday, Fisk remarked, "Are you kidding? He could tear up this league right now." But Frank still had to wait. Yes, waiting for a call to play in the major leagues was a lot harder than just waiting for a good pitch to hit. And even though Frank always knew he had to work hard and wait for his chance, this time was especially hard. It was a lot like not getting drafted all over again, like getting cut from the Olympic team all over again. "I thought I deserved to open the 1990 season in Chicago, no questions asked," Frank insisted. "When I didn't make it, my first reaction was anger. That's when my father had a talk with me." Frank Sr.'s advice was simple: "Don't go down there and sulk," he said. "Just do what you've been doing since you picked up a bat: Hit the ball."

# 6

# The Show

FRANK TOOK HIS father's advice and went to work. In one of his first minor league games, Frank was with his Birmingham team for a game in Chattanooga, Tennessee. On the first pitch he faced, Frank drilled what people estimated to be the second-longest home run ever at Engel Field, a 480-foot drive to left-center field. Only Harmon Killebrew, now a major league Hall-of-Famer, had ever hit a ball there that traveled further. By the beginning of August, Frank was leading the league in slugging percentage, on-base percentage, runs scored, and bases on balls.

The White Sox front office was so excited about Frank's exploits, it seemed they always started their mornings by talking about what their phenom had done in Birmingham the previous night. "It got to the point where nobody ever used his last name," Danny Evans, the White Sox Director of Player Personnel, said. "Every morning, our people would ask, 'What did Frank do last night?'"

Finally, they decided it was time to make a move. When Frank arrived at the park early on August 2, a coach told him to clean out his locker. "You're on your way to The Show," he said. Thomas couldn't believe it. The White Sox were playing a road game against the Brewers that night, and Frank would finally get his chance to play in a major league game.

Frank arrived at County Stadium shortly before the first game of a twi-night doubleheader. For a while, things didn't go very well for Frank, who was very nervous in his first game and failed to get a hit in four at bats.

It isn't unusual for even the best players to struggle when they first play in the major leagues. Ryne Sandberg, the Chicago Cubs' all-star second baseman for many years, managed one hit in his first 32 trips to the plate. Even Hall-of-Famer Willie Mays needed 27 at bats to get his second hit.

The next day, Frank bounced back strongly, stroking a triple that drove home the winning run. It was the first of seven straight games in which Frank had a hit. He struck out only once in his first 28 at bats for Chicago.

Frank's personality also made a favorable impression on his new teammates. Bobby Thigpen, the club's star relief pitcher, was impressed with Frank's modesty. "He has a lot of confidence, and that's good, very good," Thigpen told a reporter from the *Chicago Tribune*, the city's largest newspaper. "But he's on the quiet side, and doesn't say much. Off the field he's not cocky or aggressive. He's the kind of guy everyone's pulling for."

Frank made sure he used his first paychecks to buy a satellite dish for his dad back home in Columbus. After every game, he could still phone his biggest fan, his father, to discuss the day's game.

Frank played in the season's final 60 games, batting a robust .330 with seven homers and 31 RBIs. He was even named American League Player of the Week in September, while he was putting together a 14-game hitting streak that helped the White Sox to a second-place finish in the AL West.

# 7

# Close Encounters

FRANK THOMAS WAS in the big leagues to stay. But he wanted to improve even more during the off-season, so he traveled from his home in Columbus all the way out to Los Angeles and spent a month hitting baseballs with established stars Eric Davis and Darryl Strawberry. In an interview with *Sports Illustrated*, Davis described what he saw in Thomas as, "Awesome, totally. You don't see many big guys with the bat speed and agility he has. The only thing that can stop Frank from having success is Frank."

Frank was even a success at making contact in restaurants. After a day game in spring training, he and a teammate, Melido Perez, were about to sit down for dinner when Frank accidentally bumped into another customer. Frank apologized to the woman and began talking to her. Before the next spring training, she became Elise Silver Thomas, Frank's wife.

Because he was still a young player, people were always testing Frank and trying to see how he would react to different situations — even bad situations. It was still early in the 1991 season when the Cleveland Indians came to visit the Sox at Comiskey Park for a four-game series. The Sox won two of the first three games and had their ace pitcher Jack McDowell on the mound for the final contest. After the Indians scored a few runs early in the game, McDowell threw a pitch that almost hit Mark Whiten, the Indians' right fielder. Whiten thought McDowell had tried to hit him, and he yelled at the pitcher almost immediately. McDowell yelled back, and soon, the two players were fighting near the pitcher's mound, while many of their teammates were pushing and shoving nearby.

The next inning, Frank came up to bat against Cleveland's Todd Stottlemyre, and sure enough, Stottlemyre's first pitch barely sailed under Frank's chin. For a few moments, there was great tension on the field. Frank was much bigger and stronger than Stottlemyre, and another fight could have been bad for both players and for their teams. Frank could have created a scene if he felt he wanted to prove something to Stottlemyre and to the Indians. But instead of charging the mound, Frank kept his cool and concentrated on his at bat. Stottlemyre walked him on the next pitch. After the game, Frank told reporters, "The game was already out of hand, and he wasn't trying to hit me."

Frank's cool and patience were becoming legendary among the other White Sox players. In an August game against the Baltimore Orioles, Frank nailed a 430-foot home run, well over the fence in left field. He trotted around the bases, accepted congratulations from his teammates and sat down on the bench in the dugout with a strange look on his face. "What's wrong?" asked Carlton Fisk. Thomas made a lunging gesture with his arms and shook his head. "That pitch was this far outside," he said. Even when Frank achieved good results from flailing at bad pitches, he kept reminding himself to swing only at the good ones.

In his first full season, Frank took enough bad pitches to lead the American League in both walks (138) and on-base percentage (.454). He also swung at enough good ones to hit 32 home runs and drive in 109 runs, while batting .318.

Again, the Sox finished second in their division, this time behind the Minnesota Twins, who would go on to win the World Series. After the season Frank finished third in the balloting for the AL's Most Valuable Player award. And even though his defense still needed work, his hitting showed such amazing maturity that it led writer Thomas Boswell of the

*Washington Post* to ask the question: "When was the last time a player, after just one full season, was widely regarded as the best hitter in baseball?" Boswell also described the way Thomas hit to all fields: "With him, it's 25 percent to left, 25 percent to center, 25 percent to right, and 25 percent to the parking lot."

# 8

# Swinging Away

FRANK'S SUCCESS IN baseball began leading to other things. Kids wanted his autograph. Companies wanted him to endorse their products. He even made a small appearance in a movie called "Mr. Baseball" with actor Tom Selleck. But by 1992, his second complete season with the Sox, Frank discovered that positive publicity could be both good and bad. Each day, Frank listened to people tell him what a good player he was. But Frank also thought it was important not to get carried away with all the compliments he was getting. So he typed the letters DBTH on a piece of tape and stuck the tape above his locker in Comiskey Park. The letters stood for "Don't Believe the Hype." They reminded him and everyone around him that Frank Thomas would not allow himself to get a big head.

Above all, Frank *worked* on his game. When people saw his short, easy, compact swing, they often thought that he was born to swing a bat. But Frank kept making things look easier because he kept working harder to make them appear that way.

Frank always gave a lot of credit to Walt Hriniak, the White Sox batting instructor, who taught Frank how to do certain things with his swing that would allow him to see the ball better and not make unnecessary movements with his arms and legs, which would keep him from swinging exactly where and when he wanted to. For one thing, Frank never had a sweeping, looping swing; his stroke was tighter and quicker than most. When reminded of Frank's swing, Auburn's Coach Baird used to say, "We never messed with his swing very much. You don't teach Picasso how to paint, but you may teach him a little about color schemes."

Still, Hriniak was convinced that Frank could be a better hitter, still, by taking his top hand off the bat just after he made contact with the baseball. The idea is that the batter is more likely to keep his head level — and his eyes on the ball — when he knows his head won't be turning to the side because of a hard swing with both arms. Reaction has been mixed over the years to the Hriniak theory of hitting. Most people feel it helps batters hit for higher average, but for less power. This was just fine with Frank, who felt he'd rather make contact more often then just hit long home runs once in a while in between strikeouts. "Walter stresses discipline, which is fine with me," Frank said. "He makes sure I keep my head down and see the ball longer."

With Hriniak's instruction, Frank would spend long hours in a net-enclosed cage taking swings at pitch after pitch. Sometimes, when a batting-practice pitcher wasn't around, Coach Hriniak would have a machine throw balls to him. In spring training, the coach even had Frank swing at practice pitches with his right hand at his side and only his left hand on the bat. Anybody who has ever swung a bat can try this for himself and see how hard it would be for Frank to do it. It's a bit like hitting with one hand tied behind your back. But Frank would swing like that for an hour, making sure he extended his left arm just the way Coach Hriniak wanted him to on every swing.

Then when he finished with the left-handed drill, Frank would put both hands on the bat and practice hitting pitches to right field for another hour. The idea is that most power hitters usually want to pull the ball. So right-handed batters will hit most pitches to left field and lefties will pull most balls to right field. Unfortunately, by concentrating on big swings that hit balls to only part of the field, some batters leave themselves vulnerable to certain pitches in certain areas, particularly curveballs that cross the outside corner of the plate.

Once a game started, Coach Hriniak also encouraged Frank to watch opposing pitchers deliver their pitches when he wasn't batting. Frank studied the point of release so that he could follow the ball out of the pitcher's hand more easily when he batted against that pitcher. "I don't like to guess at the pitch," Frank would say; "I like to adjust to whatever it is and be ready for it. If I like it, I'll swing."

Hriniak's reaction after working with Frank for less than a year was almost one of amazement: "I've seen power hitters before, but never anyone who understood hitting like Frank," Hriniak said. "The last guy like him was Ted Williams." "The Splendid Splinter," as Williams was known, is considered by many people to be the greatest hitter of all time. In 1941, he hit for a .406 average, the last time a major league player hit over .400.

Frank is a nice guy off the field. But because of his ability to crush a baseball the way few players ever have, Frank has earned the nickname "The Big Hurt." Even Tim Raines, Frank's teammate, confessed, "Frank is like Dr. Jekyll and Mr. Hyde. Off the field he's sweet and nice; on the field, you should hear some of the things he says about himself after a strikeout."

A reporter once asked Frank about the nickname. How was it, the man wanted to know, that a player who had been over-looked by scouts, cut from teams by coaches and told to wait even by those who believed in him . . . just how did he become good enough to be called The Big Hurt? Frank thought for a minute. He thought about the day he wasn't picked in the draft, about the day he was cut from the Olympic team, and about the day the White Sox sent him to Birmingham when he felt he should have gone to Chicago. Then he looked up and answered, "I guess you could say a lot of little hurts went into making The Big Hurt."

There could have been another disappointment in Frank's

career that summer, when he wasn't selected to play in the All-Star game. There he was, third in the AL's MVP voting the previous year, and hitting .306 with 13 homers and 57 RBIs at the midway point of 1992 — but American League manager Tony LaRussa passed him by. Frank could have been very upset about this setback, too, but instead, he took it as a blessing. His wife Elise gave birth to their son Sterling during the break, and Frank was by her side. "I watched the game on the hospital TV and I was holding Sterling in my arms," Frank remembered. "See, there's a reason for everything."

For the Sox, there was reason for disappointment. Of course, Frank had another fine year; led the league in extra-base hits (72), on-base percentage (.439), walks (122), and doubles (46), and was near the top in almost every other offensive category. He recorded his first five-hit game during a career-high 19-game hitting streak. But the Sox fell to third place in their first season with Gene Lamont as manager. Chicago hadn't won its division now since 1983.

# 9

# Getting Defensive

FRANK WAS DETERMINED to work on his defense, the only weak part of his game. During spring training in 1993, he'd rise early and arrive at the field in Sarasota at 7:30 to start fielding ground balls on his own. Then when the pitchers arrived at 10:30, he'd join them in regular infield drills. As hard as Frank worked with his bat, he worked even harder with his glove. During the first month of the season, Frank made a defensive play that looked astounding for a man who was supposed to be an average first baseman. First, he dived to his right to smother a hard-hit ground ball. Then he got to his feet and fired a strike to his catcher, who tagged out an opposing runner at home plate. Later, Frank called that play his favorite moment of the season. "I couldn't have made that play last year," Frank said at the time. "I worked all spring to be able to do that."

On September 19, as the Sox were in Oakland, Frank chased a foul pop-up that had been hit over his head. He missed the ball and crashed into the railing in front of the stands. He tried to play with the bump on his elbow for a few days, but soon realized that he had to sit out a few games in order to allow his bruised triceps to heal properly. He slept with his arm in a sling for three uncomfortable nights. When he returned to the lineup, the White Sox used him as a designated hitter, so he wouldn't have to play in the field. The Sox clinched their first division title in ten years with a week to go in the regular season. Now the main thing was to get Frank ready for the upcoming playoff series against the Toronto Blue Jays.

Still, there was also the issue of which player would lead the American League in runs batted in. Both Frank and Albert

79

Belle of the Cleveland Indians entered the season's final weekend tied for the lead with 126. As fate would have it, the White Sox were in Cleveland for their final weekend series. Frank didn't play in either of the first two games. Belle, meanwhile, drove in two runs on Friday and one more on Saturday, giving him 129 RBIs going into the final game. Belle went 0-for-4 in that game, and was stuck on 129. Frank kept things interesting when his double to right-center drove home a run in the first and his single to left knocked in another in the sixth. Frank, now only one RBI behind Belle, had one more at bat in the eighth inning. The Sox had a man on first with one out, and since the game really didn't affect either team in the standings, Frank was willing to be extra aggressive at the plate to see if he could knock in the run, or even pick up two RBIs with a home run. But the Indians pitched very carefully to Frank and never gave him a good pitch to hit. After Frank took ball four and started trotting to first base, even the Cleveland fans started booing the pitcher.

Still, Frank's 128 RBIs set a new club record, and he also established franchise standards for home runs (41), sacrifice flies (13), extra base hits (77), and slugging percentage (.607) in a single season.

# 10

# Postseason

THERE WAS MORE work to be done. The White Sox were in the playoffs for the first time in ten years, and they would face the Toronto Blue Jays, the team that had won the World Series the previous year and was favored to win again. Frank's elbow was still giving him trouble — so much trouble that Manager Lamont decided to use him as Chicago's designated hitter rather than its first baseman for the first two games of the best-of-seven series. The Sox lost both games at Comiskey Park, by scores of 7–3 and 3–1.

Frank wasn't his old self. Because of his injury, he was having trouble swinging a bat, and his teammates were feeling pressure to pick up the slack. As the series moved to Toronto, the Sox put the sock back into their bats. They won the next two games, 6–1 and 7–4, as Frank homered in the fourth game. Although the Blue Jays were too strong, finishing off the Sox with back-to-back victories, Frank did more than his fair share, finishing the series with a .353 batting average and ten walks in the six games.

Several weeks after the Blue Jays won their second World Series, the baseball writers were set to announce their selection as the American League's Most Valuable Player for the regular season. Many people felt that the award would either go to Frank or one of two Blue Jays, first baseman John Olerud, who had led the AL in batting, or designated hitter Paul Molitor. Frank slept for two hours thinking about the telephone call he hoped he'd receive the next day. When he heard the first ring, Frank didn't wait for a second one. He answered right away, hoping enough of the 28 writers who were voting would select

Frank as their top choice for the award. The news was better than he could have imagined. Not only did Frank win the award, he received first-place votes from all 28 writers, becoming only the eighth American Leaguer, and tenth player from either league, to win the award by unanimous vote.

Still, as great as Frank was on the field in 1993, he did some of his best work off the field. Frank remembered the work his father did in the Columbus community, and wanted to do some of the same things around Chicago. To honor his sister Pamela, Frank started the Frank Thomas Charitable Foundation, an organization that contributes regularly to the Leukemia Society of America and other good causes that try to help people in need. "Maybe one day we can do something about cancer," Frank said. "I want to see the day when the doctors can knock this thing out."

Frank also began visiting high schools in the Chicago area as part of baseball's Stay in School program. During these visits he talks to students about what it was like when he was their age, about his close family, about the importance his parents placed on his classwork and homework. He also explains that sometimes the setbacks in his life have actually helped him. When no team picked him in the 1986 Amateur Draft for instance, it gave Frank a chance to attend college and to hone his baseball skills at a high level while he attained a college education.

# 11

# Striking Connections

EVEN AFTER FRANK'S spectacular 1993 MVP season, the biggest news in the Sox's spring training camp wasn't about him; it was about another player who, like Frank, had excelled in another sport besides baseball. Only this player was the greatest basketball player in the world. This new member of the White Sox organization was Michael Jordan.

Jordan had left the Chicago Bulls the previous year after having led the team to three straight NBA titles. Now, he wanted to try his hand at baseball, a sport he hadn't played in years. For that reason, some players resented Jordan's appearance in spring training and felt that it was an unnecessary publicity stunt. Still, Frank and Michael took an immediate liking to one another. Frank appreciated the fact that Michael wanted to try a new challenge, especially when it would have been easy for him to go back to being the best player in basketball as opposed to a baseball player with a lot to learn. So when Michael needed batting advice, Frank helped him.

The two remained friends, even though the White Sox sent Jordan down to Birmingham, where Frank had started the season four years earlier. Unfortunately, baseball didn't come nearly as easily as basketball for Michael, who would have to spend the entire year playing for the Double-A team.

At least the minor leagues played a full season; the major league season was short-circuited when the players went on strike in a dispute with the team owners over money-related issues. The timing could not have been worse for players such as Houston's Jeff Bagwell, Seattle's Ken Griffey Jr., San Francisco's Matt Williams, and Frank. Each was having a great year with a chance to accomplish extraordinary things. Frank had a chance to lead the league in batting average, home runs, and RBIs, baseball's Triple Crown. Nobody has done that in either league since Boston's Carl Yastrzemski turned the trick in 1967.

The White Sox were also leading the league's newly formed Central Division by one game.

Despite the strike, 1994 marked the fourth straight season in which Frank batted at least .300 and recorded over 20 home runs, 100 runs, 100 RBIs, and 100 walks in the same season. Only three other players, all Hall-of-Famers, have ever matched that feat: Babe Ruth, Lou Gehrig, and Ted Williams.

At the end of the shortened season, Frank was the astonishing career leader among all active major-league players in both on-base percentage (.441) and slugging percentage (.561).

He also hit a double at the MVP plate, earning 24 of 28 first-place votes to win the award for a second straight season. Seattle's Ken Griffey Jr. received three and Cleveland's Belle the other. "I'm very happy," said Thomas after hearing the news, "but it's kind of bittersweet, too. Individual awards don't mean anything if you don't win anything as a team. I don't have a World Series ring on my finger, and I could be playing in my first right now."

But instead of swinging for the fences at a major-league park in October, Frank was in a batting cage taking swings at tomatoes and grapefruit that Late Night talkshow host David Letterman was pitching to him. That was a fun diversion for Frank, but he would rather have been playing the real thing.

But as he had done before in his life many times, Frank would have to be patient. It was like waiting for his pitch, waiting for his call to the Big Leagues. Frank Thomas doesn't mind waiting, because he knows that the best is yet to come.

# Sources

*The Associated Press*
*Auburn University Athletic Department*
*The Boston Globe*
*CNN*
*The Chicago Tribune*
*ESPN*
*The Los Angeles Times*
*Major League Baseball*
*People*
*The Sporting News*
*Sports Illustrated*
*Sports Illustrated for Kids*
*The New York Times*
*The Seattle Times*
*USA Today*
*The Washington Post*

If you want to write to the author, address your letter to:

> East End Publishing
> 54 Alexander Dr.
> Syosset, NY 11791

All letters that require an answer *must* include a self-addressed and stamped envelope.

If you want to write to Ken Griffey Jr., address your letter to:

> Ken Griffey Jr.
> c/o Seattle Mariners
> 83 S. King St. – Suite 300
> Seattle, WA 98104

If you want to write to Frank Thomas, address your letter to:

> Frank Thomas
> c/o Chicago White Sox
> Comiskey Park
> 333 W. 35th St.
> Chicago, IL 60616

# GEORGE KENNETH GRIFFEY JR.

Birthdate: November 21, 1969

Birthplace: Donora, Pennsylvania

Height: 6-3

Weight: 205

## MINOR LEAGUE STATS

| YEAR/TEAM | G | AB | R | H | 2B | 3B | HR | RBI | SB | SLG | BB | SO | AVG |
|---|---|---|---|---|---|---|---|---|---|---|---|---|---|
| '87/Bellingham | 54 | 182 | 43 | 57 | 9 | 1 | 14 | 44 | 13 | .604 | 44 | 42 | .313 |
| '88/San Bernard. | 58 | 219 | 50 | 74 | 13 | 3 | 11 | 42 | 32 | .575 | 34 | 39 | .338 |
| '88/Vermont | 17 | 61 | 10 | 17 | 5 | 1 | 2 | 10 | 4 | .492 | 5 | 12 | .279 |
| TOTALS | 129 | 462 | 103 | 148 | 27 | 5 | 27 | 96 | 49 | .576 | 83 | 93 | .320 |

## MAJOR LEAGUE STATS

| YEAR/TEAM | G | AB | R | H | 2B | 3B | HR | RBI | SB | SLG | BB | SO | AVG |
|---|---|---|---|---|---|---|---|---|---|---|---|---|---|
| '89/Seattle | 127 | 455 | 61 | 120 | 23 | 0 | 16 | 61 | 16 | .420 | 44 | 83 | .264 |
| '90/Seattle | 155 | 597 | 91 | 179 | 28 | 7 | 22 | 80 | 16 | .481 | 63 | 81 | .300 |
| '91/Seattle | 154 | 548 | 76 | 179 | 42 | 1 | 22 | 100 | 18 | .527 | 71 | 82 | .327 |
| '92/Seattle | 142 | 565 | 83 | 174 | 39 | 4 | 27 | 103 | 10 | .535 | 44 | 67 | .323 |
| '93/Seattle | 156 | 582 | 113 | 180 | 38 | 3 | 45 | 109 | 17 | .617 | 96 | 91 | .308 |
| '94/Seattle | 111 | 433 | 94 | 140 | 24 | 4 | 40 | 90 | 11 | .674 | 56 | 73 | .309 |
| TOTALS | 845 | 3180 | 518 | 972 | 194 | 19 | 172 | 543 | 88 | .541 | 374 | 477 | .306 |

# FRANK EDWARD THOMAS JR.

Birthdate: May 27, 1968

Birthplace: Columbus, Georgia

Height: 6-5

Weight: 257

## AUBURN UNIVERSITY STATS

| YEAR/TEAM | G | AB | R | H | 2B | 3B | HR | RBI | SB | SLG | BB | SO | AVG |
|---|---|---|---|---|---|---|---|---|---|---|---|---|---|
| '87/Auburn | 59 | 209 | 56 | 75 | 12 | 0 | 21 | 68 | 0 | .718 | 38 | 36 | .359 |
| '88/Auburn | 55 | 182 | 45 | 70 | 21 | 0 | 9 | 54 | 4 | .637 | 42 | 22 | .385 |
| '89/Auburn | 64 | 206 | 62 | 83 | 19 | 3 | 19 | 83 | 0 | .801 | 73 | 25 | .403 |
| TOTALS | 178 | 597 | 163 | 228 | 52 | 3 | 49 | 205 | 4 | .725 | 153 | 83 | .382 |

## MINOR LEAGUE STATS

| YEAR/TEAM | G | AB | R | H | 2B | 3B | HR | RBI | SB | SLG | BB | SO | AVG |
|---|---|---|---|---|---|---|---|---|---|---|---|---|---|
| '89/Sara. (GCL) | 16 | 48 | 7 | 16 | 5 | 0 | 1 | 11 | 4 | .500 | 10 | 24 | .333 |
| '89/Sara. (FSL) | 55 | 188 | 27 | 52 | 9 | 1 | 4 | 30 | 0 | .399 | 31 | 33 | .277 |
| '90/Birm. | 109 | 353 | 84 | 114 | 27 | 5 | 18 | 71 | 7 | .581 | 112 | 74 | .323 |
| TOTALS | 180 | 589 | 118 | 182 | 41 | 6 | 23 | 112 | 11 | .516 | 153 | 131 | .309 |

## MAJOR LEAGUE STATS

| YEAR/TEAM | G | AB | R | H | 2B | 3B | HR | RBI | SB | SLG | BB | SO | AVG |
|---|---|---|---|---|---|---|---|---|---|---|---|---|---|
| '90/Chicago | 60 | 191 | 39 | 63 | 11 | 3 | 7 | 31 | 0 | .529 | 44 | 54 | .330 |
| '91/Chicago | 158 | 559 | 104 | 178 | 31 | 2 | 32 | 109 | 1 | .553 | 138 | 112 | .318 |
| '92/Chicago | 160 | 573 | 108 | 185 | 46 | 2 | 24 | 115 | 6 | .536 | 122 | 88 | .323 |
| '93/Chicago | 153 | 549 | 106 | 174 | 36 | 0 | 41 | 128 | 4 | .609 | 112 | 54 | .317 |
| '94/Chicago | 113 | 399 | 106 | 141 | 34 | 1 | 38 | 101 | 2 | .729 | 109 | 61 | .353 |
| TOTALS | 644 | 2271 | 463 | 741 | 158 | 8 | 142 | 484 | 13 | .590 | 525 | 369 | .326 |

If you enjoyed this book you might want to order some of our other exciting titles:

BASKETBALL SUPERSTARS ALBUM 1995, Richard J. Brenner. Includes 16 full-color pages, and mini-bios of the game's top superstars, plus career and all time stats. 48 pages ($4.50/$5.50 Can.)

SHAQUILLE O'NEAL * LARRY JOHNSON, by Richard J. Brenner. A dual biography of the two brightest young stars in basketball. 96 pages, 10 pages of photos. ($3.50/$4.50 Can.)

MICHAEL JORDAN * MAGIC JOHNSON, by Richard J. Brenner. A dual biography of two of the greatest superstars of all time. 128 pages, 15 dynamite photos. ($3.50/$4.25 Can.)

TROY AIKMAN * STEVE YOUNG, by Richard J. Brenner. A dual biography of the top two quarterbacks in the NFL. 96 pages, 10 pages of photos. ($3.50/$4.50 Can.)

BARRY BONDS * ROBERTO ALOMAR, by Bob Woods. A dual biography of two of the brightest stars in baseball. 96 pages, 10 pages of photos. ($3.50/$4.50 Can.)

MARIO LEMIEUX, by Richard J. Brenner. An exciting biography of one of hockey's all time greats. 96 pages, 10 pages of photos. ($3.50/$4.50 Can.)

THE WORLD SERIES, THE GREAT CONTESTS, by Richard J. Brenner. The special excitement of the Fall Classic is brought to life through seven of the most thrilling Series ever played, including 1993. 176 pages, including 16 action-packed photos. ($3.50/$4.50 Can.)

THE COMPLETE SUPER BOWL STORY, GAMES I-XXVIII, by Richard J. Brenner. The most spectacular moments in Super Bowl history are brought to life, game by game. 224 pages, including 16 memorable photos. ($4.00/$5.00 Can.)

SHAQUILLE O'NEAL, by Richard J. Brenner. An easy-to-read, photo-filled biography especially for younger readers. 32 pages. ($3.25/$4.50 Can.)

MICHAEL JORDAN, by Richard J. Brenner. An easy-to-read, photo-filled biography especially for younger readers. 32 pages. ($3.50/$4.50 Can.)

WAYNE GRETZKY, by Richard J. Brenner. An easy-to-read, photo-filled biography of hockey's greatest player. 32 pages. Revised edition. ($3.25/$4.50 Can.)

**PLEASE SEE NEXT PAGE FOR ORDER FORM**

# ORDER FORM

Payment must accompany all orders. All payments must be in U.S. dollars. Postage and handling is $1.35 per book up to a maximum of $6.75 ($1.75 to a maximum of $8.75 in Canada).

Please send me _____ total books as per the following:

❑ BASKETBALL SUPERSTARS ALBUM 1995
❑ SHAQUILLE O'NEAL * LARRY JOHNSON
❑ MICHAEL JORDAN * MAGIC JOHNSON
❑ TROY AIKMAN * STEVE YOUNG
❑ BARRY BONDS * ROBERTO ALOMAR
❑ MARIO LEMIEUX
❑ THE WORLD SERIES, THE GREAT CONTESTS
❑ THE COMPLETE SUPER BOWL STORY, GAMES I-XXVIII
❑ SHAQUILLE O'NEAL
❑ MICHAEL JORDAN
❑ WAYNE GRETZKY

PRICE OF BOOKS            $_____
POSTAGE AND HANDLING      $_____
TOTAL PAYMENT ENCLOSED    $_____

NAME _____

ADDRESS _____

CITY_____STATE _____ ZIP CODE:_____

COUNTRY_____

Send to: East End Publishing, Ltd., 54 Alexander Drive, Syosset, NY 11791 USA. Dept. WGB. Allow three weeks for delivery. Discounts are available on orders of 25 or more copies. For details, call (516) 364-6383.